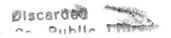

Usher

by Z.B. Hill

Superstars of Hip-Hop

Usher

by Z.B. Hill

Mason Crest

Usher

Mason Crest
370 Reed Road
Broomall, Pennsylvania 19008
www.masoncrest.com

Printed and bound in the United States of America.

First printing
9 8 7 6 5 4 3 2 1

Library of Congress Cataloging-in-Publication Data

Hill, Z. B.
  Usher / Z.B. Hill.
      p. cm. – (Superstars of hip-hop)
  Includes index.
  ISBN 978-1-4222-2531-8 (hard cover) – ISBN 978-1-4222-2508-0 (series hardcover) – ISBN 978-1-4222-9233-4 (ebook)
 1. Usher–Juvenile literature. 2. Rhythm and blues musicians–United States–Biography–Juvenile literature. 3. Singers–United States–Biography–Juvenile literature. I. Title.
  ML3930.U84H55 2012
  782.421643092–dc23
  [B]
                        2011019650

Produced by Harding House Publishing Services, Inc.
www.hardinghousepages.com
Interior Design by MK Bassett-Harvey.
Cover design by Torque Advertising & Design.

Publisher's notes:
• All quotations in this book come from original sources and contain the spelling and grammatical inconsistencies of the original text.
• The Web sites mentioned in this book were active at the time of publication. The publisher is not responsible for Web sites that have changed their addresses or discontinued operation since the date of publication. The publisher will review and update the Web site addresses each time the book is reprinted.

DISCLAIMER: The following story has been thoroughly researched, and to the best of our knowledge, represents a true story. While every possible effort has been made to ensure accuracy, the publisher will not assume liability for damages caused by inaccuracies in the data, and makes no warranty on the accuracy of the information contained herein. This story has not been authorized nor endorsed by Usher.

Contents

Hip-Hop lingo

R&B stands for "rhythm and blues." It's a kind of music that African Americans made popular in the 1940s. It has a very strong beat. Today, it's a style of music that's a lot like hip-hop.

Billboard is a magazine that keeps track of which songs are most popular.

Passion is a strong feeling for a certain activity or thing that drives you to act on its behalf.

Talent contests are where people perform for judges. The best performer wins a prize.

Potential is someone's power to do something that he hasn't done yet.

Mainstream music is music enjoyed by almost everyone.

Gospel is a type of music that started in African American churches.

Funk is a style of music started in the 1960s. It has a strong beat and is often used as dance music.

A person who **auditioned** sang or performed for someone to see if that person liked his work and wanted to give him a job.

A **contract** is a written agreement between two people. Once you've signed a contract, it's against the law to break it. When a musician signs a contract with a music company, the musician promises to give all his music to that company for them to produce as CDs and then sell—and the music company promises to pay the musician a certain amount of money. Usually, a contract is for a certain period of time.

A **vocalist** is a singer.

A **single** is one song taken from an album and sold by itself.

A **producer** is the person who oversees the creation of an album.

An album goes **gold** when it sells more than 500,000 copies.

Chapter 1

A Boy Becomes a Star

The year is 2004. Usher has just released another hit album. *Rolling Stone* calls him an "**R&B** teen dream." A few magazines say he's "the sexiest man alive." The awards are starting to come in, too. **Billboard** gives him eleven awards. He's on top of the world. He's just twenty-six years old, but he's been making music for over fifteen years!

How did it all begin? Where did this star come from? Usher says on his website, "I have been building my career since I was a little boy. Singing had always been what I wanted to do. . . . It's my biggest **passion** and my biggest joy."

Today, Usher has made his dreams come true. But it wasn't easy. He came a long way to get where he is today.

Childhood

Usher was born on October 14, 1978, in Dallas, Texas. His full name is Usher Raymond IV. He is named after his dad, Usher Raymond III.

Usher's music career began by singing in church choirs directed by his mother, J-Pat. Today, Usher, his mother, and younger brother James remain close. In this photo, J-Pat and James are shown at the launch party for Usher's "Truth Tour."

His parents had no idea their son would go on to make the name "Usher" so famous.

Sadness visited Usher's life early. When he was one year old, his parents divorced. His mom, Jonetta Patton, moved them to Chattanooga, Tennessee. Jonetta was also known as "J-Pat." Usher would never really know his real dad.

In Tennessee, J-Pat married another man. J-Pat had a baby with her new husband, and they called him James. Now Usher had a stepfather and a baby brother. It was the start of a whole new family.

Usher's mom was a musical person. Early on, she noticed her oldest son liked singing. So she put him in the church choir when he was just six years old. As it turned out, this boy could really sing! At age nine, he entered **talent contests**. And by the time he was eleven, he had won a contest. He was very proud. He was only in middle school, and the contest had high school kids in it. He had beaten kids who were many years older than him!

But this was only the beginning. Usher had a lot more awards headed his way. No one knew that better than Usher's mom. J-Pat wanted her to son to succeed. She saw great **potential** in him. She also saw that Usher needed a bigger city where he could really shine. So she made a decision. She moved herself and her two boys to Atlanta, Georgia.

J-Pat kept pushing Usher to succeed. She got a job leading a choir in Atlanta. She pushed him to enter more talent contests. When he was twelve, he joined a local R&B group called NuBeginnings.

The Hip-Hop Scene

As Usher grew up in the 1980s, hip-hop grew up, too. Hip-hop began in the 1970s. At first, it was mostly just music for the inner city.

But by the time Usher was ten or eleven, hip-hop went **mainstream**. Hip-hop record companies looked for new talent. Hip-hop was a mix of many types of music. It blended **gospel**, R&B, and **funk**. It fit Usher's young voice well.

Fame Comes Early

His hard work finally paid off. Usher met an important person at one of the Atlanta talent contests. His name was Bryan Reid. Bryan was the brother of L.A. Reid, the owner of LaFace Records. Bryan liked what he heard from Usher. He wanted his brother to meet the young man. So in 1992, when Usher was only fourteen years old, he **auditioned** for LaFace Records.

L.A. Reid was impressed. He liked Usher so much that he signed a **contract** with him! It was an amazing time for someone so young. Only fourteen years old, and his career had already begun.

One success came after another. The next year, Usher went on the TV show *Star Search*. In the show, kids with talent compete against each other. Usher competed against other male singers. And he won! He won the award for Best Teen Male **Vocalist**.

Winning *Star Search* really sped things up. Usher was quickly on his way to fame. He was asked to make a song for the movie *Poetic Justice*. The song was called "Call Me a Mack." It became Usher's first **single**.

Puff Daddy

In 1994, Usher was hard at work on his first album, simply called *Usher*. The album's **producer** was one of the biggest names in hip-hop: Sean "Puffy" Combs. He's best known as Puff Daddy (or P. Diddy.)

Puffy taught the young man a lot. He brought Usher to live with him in New York City. He wanted to guide his career toward suc-

While he was working on his first album, Usher lived with Sean "Puff Daddy" Combs (together again in this 2002 photo), probably the most influential music producer of the time. Though they didn't agree on everything, it was a learning time for the sixteen-year-old musician.

cess. He wanted to help him become a star. Puffy had been a big star himself. He was a great musician. Puffy told *People* magazine: "Usher became like a little brother to me. I got to see all of his talents. He's easy to work with, he listens, he's an incredible singer and an excellent dancer."

Usher's New Image

It wasn't all fun between Usher and Puffy. They didn't always agree. In fact, Usher sometimes felt Puffy didn't understand him. He felt like Puffy pushed him too hard. Puffy wanted a certain image for Usher. He wanted him to look like a tough guy. He didn't want him to smile in pictures. He gave him a "bad boy" image.

But Usher didn't like it. It didn't feel right. He just wanted to be himself! He told *People* magazine: "Cool guys smile."

Hard Times

But Usher and Puffy had bigger problems than image to deal with. In the middle of recording his first album, Usher's voice changed! Usher was a teenager. As boys grow into adults, their voices change. It's a normal thing to happen. But that didn't make Usher feel any better. He couldn't sing some of the notes in his songs. When he tried to hit them, his voice cracked. Or sometimes he couldn't hit the notes at all.

Some voice coaches tried to help him. But even then, Usher felt really bad. He felt like he had failed. To make things worse, his skin changed too. He got lots of pimples on his face. This too was normal for a teenager. His mom told *Teen People*: "His whole face just broke out because he was so nervous."

It's hard to picture Usher with pimples. But it's true. His whole body seemed to reject him. Also, he was far from home and lonely.

He dealt with the normal stuff that teens go through. He also dealt with a new hip-hop career. It was a lot for a young man.

But he didn't give up. He struggled through his voice and body problems. And in 1994, his album *Usher* was released.

What Next?

What was next for Usher? Everything. He was just getting started. A single from *Usher* made the top-ten charts. It was called "Think of You." It went **gold** and sold more than 500,000 copies. The future was already bright.

And yet the road wouldn't be an easy one. His record company wanted him to sell more albums. Puffy couldn't help him because he needed to work on his own career. Plus, Usher was still only sixteen years old. He still had to finish high school back in Atlanta! He had the worries of both a kid and an adult.

But his rise to stardom had begun. He wasn't going to give up now.

Hip-Hop lingo

A **jingle** is a short song written for a television commercial.

A **tutor** is someone who helps a student learn.

To **co-write** something means to write it with another person.

Ballads are slow songs that often build up to powerful endings.

An album goes **platinum** when it sells more than 1,000,000 copies.

Going **on tour** means traveling around to play your music for people at concerts.

To **open** for another musician means to play your music before the other person goes on stage.

Tear gas burns the eyes and lungs. Sometimes the police use it to control riots.

The **NAACP** is a group that works for equal rights for African Americans.

Chapter 2

Taking It to the Next Level

In some ways, Usher was already a star. He had made a hit single. People knew his name. But LaFace Records wasn't impressed yet. They thought Usher could do better. And he was up to the challenge! He was becoming a man, and now he had gotten control of his new voice. The whole world was his for the taking.

Gift of a Song

By now, people knew Usher had a great voice. The same year his first album came out, he teamed up with lots of other musicians. He sang a song called "U Will Know" for the movie *Jason's Lyric*. He joined other male singers to make the song. They called themselves Black Men United.

The next year, Usher sang with his friend Monica. She was a young, popular singer just like Usher. They made a song called "Let's Straighten It Out." And later that year, he made a song for Coca-Cola! It became a **jingle** for a TV ad.

Finishing School

Usher was very busy now. He barely had any free time. But somehow he found time to finish school. It was hard for him to think about school sometimes. After all, he was famous. He had money and a promising career. But he got a **tutor** anyway. The tutor helped him catch up on missed schoolwork. With his help, Usher finished high school.

The Next Album

LaFace Records gave Usher another chance. His first album hadn't sold as much as they wanted it to. They hoped his second would do better. It was a lot of pressure for a young man. To help him, LaFace gave Usher some of the best producers in hip-hop. Babyface, Teddy Riley, and Jermaine Dupri would work with Usher on the new album.

The three producers knew a lot about music. But they let Usher speak his mind. They wanted to hear what the young singer thought about life and music. In the end, Usher **co-wrote** six of the album's nine songs. He proved he had talents besides singing. He wrote about growing from a teenager into a man. That's why he called it *My Way*. The second album was done Usher's way.

My Way was a big hit. People loved the new album. Monica teamed up with Usher again to make the song "Slow Jam" for the album. The album had a lot of **ballads**. People really liked it when Usher slowed his music down.

Then there were Jermaine Dupri's songs. These were some of the best. Dupri helped Usher make the songs "You Make Me Wanna..." and "Nice and Slow." In the end, "You Make Me Wanna . . ." went **platinum**. It spent fourteen weeks in the number-one spot. In 1998, *My Way* was the eleventh best-selling album. Usher had arrived. He was truly a hip-hop star.

Going on Tour

It was time to take the music to the people. It was time to go **on tour**. Before Usher could do that, he needed to work on his moves. Today Usher is famous for his live shows. People know him as an amazing dancer. But he didn't get there without hard work. Back in 1997, he started practicing his dance moves.

People loved it. Usher's moves were smooth, and his voice was strong. He **opened** for Puff Daddy and Mary J. Blige, two of the biggest names in hip-hop! It was a big honor.

In 1996, Usher had the chance to work with another of hip-hop's superstar producers and writers, Jermaine Dupri (shown here with Usher in 2004). Jermaine's songs finally brought Usher the success he had worked for since childhood.

Usher toured for the first time in 1997. A choreographer worked with him to polish his dancing, and he opened for Puff Daddy, Mary J. Blige, and Janet Jackson. Crowds everywhere wildly greeted the new star.

Taking the Stage

Usher loves to perform at live shows. Believe it or not, though, he still gets nervous. But he does have a way to deal with it. He told *J-14* magazine, "I get ten bags of M&Ms and spill them on a table. Then I sort them out into little piles of all the same color. It takes a while, but it does the trick!"

Practice also helps keep Usher calm. He spends hours and hours practicing his moves. He has a few famous dancers he admires. He tries to be like them. His dance heroes include old-time dancers Fred Astaire and Gene Kelly. But he also loves Michael Jackson.

Dancing is very hard work. Usher has to keep his body very fit. Otherwise, it's too dangerous! During dance practice for his 1999 tour, Usher hurt his shoulder badly. He ended up having to cancel the shows. That's how serious dancing can be.

There are other dangers, too. While on tour in 1998, someone in the crowd opened a can of **tear gas**. No one was seriously hurt. Usher hadn't even taken the stage yet. So he was all right too. But he learned a lesson that day. He had to be careful.

Even friendly fans can be hard on Usher. Wherever he goes, people know who he is. He never has any privacy. He can't even go to the bathroom without someone saying, "Hey! That's Usher!"

When you're famous, people are always watching. They see your best and worst moments. Usher won a Grammy award in 1997. It was his job to say the name of the next winner of an award. The winner was a rock & roll star, Bob Dylan. Usher messed up and called him "Bill" by mistake.

TV to Big Screen

The late 1990s were busy years for Usher. He wasn't just touring and making music. He was also building an acting career. His first

Usher broke into acting in 1997. His first role was as Jeremy, Moesha's boyfriend on the television series of the same name. The title character was played by Brandy, another top musical talent. This was just the beginning of Usher's acting career.

role was in a TV show called *Moesha*. It starred the pop singer Brandy. Usher played her boyfriend, Jeremy.

Usher proved he had some acting skills. He got offered more and more TV jobs. In June of 1998, he was in eight episodes of the show *The Bold and the Beautiful*. The **NAACP** gave him an Image Award for his work. The award was a huge honor. It's given to performers who create a positive image of black Americans.

Now Usher's acting career was really moving fast. That same year he got a part in his first movie. It was called *The Faculty*. Usher played a high school student whose body gets taken over by aliens. The movie offers kept coming. The next year, he got a part in popular movie called *She's All That*.

Movie Star

But nothing compared to his star role in the movie *Light It Up*. Usher's old friend Babyface produced it. Usher played a teen named Lester. Lester tries to make his rundown high school a better place. The movie was a big step up for the young actor. It was a chance to really shine. And Usher definitely shone bright.

One producer said this about Usher: "Usher turned out to be a real actor. . . . He was very committed to the film and to understanding his role. Lester is a difficult part. But Usher really got the character and played it beautifully."

Usher took acting seriously. He wasn't just a singer who happened to act. He wanted to be a truly good actor. He told Fox Movies, "I've always loved music. But there's so much more to being an entertainer than singing and dancing. To be a triple threat you have to have the acting. So I figured I'll take that step. And *Light It Up* gave me the chance to really get into it."

The producers of *Light It Up* asked Usher to make a song for the movie soundtrack. Usher said no. He wanted to be taken seriously for his acting. In other words, he didn't want people to think he got the part just because of his singing skills.

Usher proved he meant what he said. Usher left his tour with Janet Jackson early so he could start filming *Light It Up*. It was a bold choice, and a hard one too. But he was right. After that, people started to take him more seriously as an actor. In 1999, he costarred in *Texas Rangers*. The movie tells the story of a group of young people. They fight to protect the West after the Civil War. Usher had to learn to ride a horse for the movie. Usher told MTV, "I got a few sores, you know, blisters from riding on those horses. Saddles are hard when you're not used to them."

Usher learned to ride a horse for the film *Texas Rangers*, the story of young people who band together to protect the West after the Civil War. The film stars (left to right) Ashton Kutcher, James Der Beek, Dylan McDermott, and Usher.

Doing It His Way

Usher couldn't be stopped. He was on a speeding train to stardom. If you turned on the TV in 1999, chances are good you saw Usher. He appeared on *The Oprah Winfrey Show*, *The Chris Rock Show*, and Nickelodeon's *Big-Help-a-Thon* and *All That*. Usher was everywhere. And he took another step to fame when he started his own record label. In 1998, he created Us Records.

Usher had learned a lot in his twenty-one years. He'd done more at his age than most people do in a lifetime. He had won riches and fame for his talents. His name was known across America.

What was next for Usher? What could he possibly do that he hadn't already done?

Well, as it turns out, there was a lot he had yet to do. Usher was still just getting started.

Hip-Hop lingo

An album is **leaked** if people start listening to it before it is available in stores.

Evolution is how someone or something changes and grows over time.

Mentors are people who teach someone else life lessons.

A **slow jam** is a song that is good for slow dancing.

Chapter 3

Top of His Game

There didn't seem to be anything Usher couldn't do. He danced, sang, acted, produced albums, and ran his own label. His energy and success earned him the nicknames "Big Ush" and "Big Tyme." He really was big in the hip-hop world. No one had as much going for them as Usher.

The Next Album

Usher's fourth album was supposed to be called *All About U*. But this was the year 2001. Music-sharing programs had just been invented. A program called Napster let users download music for free. So when Usher's new album **leaked** to Napster, he was upset. Musicians didn't know how to feel about Napster. It felt wrong for people to hear your music before you even finish working on it. Plus, you don't get paid for the music people download!

So Usher went back to the studio. He recorded some fresh songs. Then he released the album with a new title: *8701*.

Usher wasn't just a superstar in the United States. His song "Pop Ya Collar" was a major hit in Europe and a number-two hit in the United Kingdom. In this 2001 photo, Usher is performing at the Music of Black Origin Awards in London.

He called it *8701* because of the day it was released: August 7, 2001. (Get it—8/7/01?) The numbers also stood for the years between 1987 and 2001. These were the years Usher had been making music. *8701* really proved Usher's talent as a singer. He spread his wings and tried some new things. He wanted to show that he was growing as an artist. This was not the boy from *Star Search*. This was a grown man.

The new album also proved that Usher was here to stay. Some hip-hop stars are only around for a few years. Not Usher. He had his sights set on long-term goals. He told IMDb.com, "The album is really about my **evolution** as an artist, as a writer, as a producer and as a man."

Usher also talked about the men who taught him the hip-hop business. "I learned how music works dealing with Jermaine Dupri. I learned how image works dealing with Puff Daddy."

8701 showed that Usher took advice from both his **mentors**. He combined Puffy's style with Dupri's music talent and added his own Usher touch. The results were good. People loved *8701*. Many of the album's singles went to number one. "Pop Ya Collar" was a huge hit in Europe. It hit number two in the United Kingdom. Back home, "U Remind Me" was a number-one hit for four weeks.

Usher also made a **slow jam** for the album called "U Got It Bad." Dupri and Brian Cox helped him write it. "U Got It Bad" stayed at number one for weeks. It was one of many songs to make the album famous. *8701* was so popular that it went platinum four times! Usher won two Grammys for the album. He won the award for "Best Male R&B Vocal" two years in a row. He is only the third singer to ever do that.

Higher and Higher

Most singers dream of their album going gold. Very few ever manage to go platinum. But Usher had done it. *8701* won just about every award possible. It made Usher a lot of money. He was truly at the top of his game. But he wasn't about to slow down.

The album *8701* made Usher part of music history. Songs from that album won Usher the Best Male R&B Vocal Grammys in consecutive years. Usher is only the third artist to win the award back to back.

He finished 2002 with a few acting jobs for TV. He was in *The Twilight Zone* and *7th Heaven*. He also played music legend Marvin Gaye in *American Dreams*. That was a big honor.

The next year, 2003, was another good one for Usher. He continued to succeed in acting and singing. But it was 2004 that really changed his life. If Usher thought he'd reached the top, he was wrong. He was going to soar even higher.

Hip-Hop lingo

Confessions are secrets that someone tells someone else.
Lyrics are the words in a song.

Chapter 4

Confessions

Usher's called his next album **Confessions**. His other albums brought him fame and fortune. *Confessions* brought him a new level of respect. Once *Confessions* was out, people around the world knew Usher's name. He truly became a global superstar. But *Confessions* was important for other reasons, too. It told how Usher really felt about things. He told Magic.com, "I'm not afraid to speak . . . about the issues men deal with. I'm telling on myself."

Relationships between men and women can be hard. And relationships were a huge part of Usher's life story. He wanted to sing about these very personal experiences. So he did. He showed his inner self to the whole world. It was a big risk for him to take.

Family

Usher's *Confessions* told stories inspired by his life. His family is a huge part of his life. To understand Usher, it's important to know a little about his family.

Usher is close to his younger half-brother, James. He's also close to his grandparents, aunts, and uncles. But he's always been closest to his mother. She was the one who first taught him music and singing. She was the one who helped him start his career. Even in difficult times, she stayed by his side. It's not hard to see why Usher loves her. "She's always been there for me," he told the Associated Press. "It always helps to have someone behind you, and my mother was that person."

In this 2005 photo, Usher and his mother are attending the premiere of *In the Mix*. J-Pat has been a major influence on Usher's career and life. She taught him music, and encouraged him to compete in talent shows, supporting him every step of the way.

Usher has an amazing mother. But he's never had a real father. For a little while, he had a stepfather. Then his mom divorced again when Usher was a teen. His real dad, Usher Raymond III, was never around. Usher didn't even see his father until his grandma's funeral. He never connected to his dad. He told *Teen People* that he didn't care. It doesn't make him angry. "I've never had a relationship with him. How can you love somebody or hate somebody you've never known?"

Musical Fathers

Usher has been lucky enough to have a lot of musical "fathers." L.A. Reid from LaFace Records became a role model for Usher. Usher told *USA Today*, "L.A. took me under his wing like a father." Puff Daddy also treated Usher like a son. They both taught Usher a lot about life. L.A. taught him about music. He taught him about old R&B singers. He opened up Usher's musical world. Puffy helped him with other things, like production. He taught him how image and style are a part of hip-hop.

Girlfriends

Women love Usher. Many buy his CDs and go to his live shows. But that doesn't mean Usher's love life is easy. In fact, it makes it much harder. He's struggled to stay with one woman.

When he was young, Usher was not a hit with the ladies. He has some painful memories from his teen years. One time, when he was at a skating rink, he tried to hold a girl's hand—but she skated away! She left him hanging. Another time, he had to move away from his girlfriend. His family was moving to Atlanta. He had to break up with her. They wouldn't see each other anymore. Usher said that it broke his heart.

Things didn't get easier when he became an adult. His love life has had ups and downs. Usher dated Rozonda "Chilli" Thomas

Dating hasn't always been easy for Usher. In 2004, he dated model Naomi Campbell, a superstar in her own right (seen here at the 2004 MTV European Music Awards). According to sources, they broke up when she refused to attend the *Billboard* awards.

from 2002 to 2004. But she accused him of cheating. Things ended badly. In 2004, Usher dated a supermodel, Naomi Campbell. That didn't work out either.

Usher seems to be really hurt by breakups. *Confessions* describes a lot of heartbreak. The song "Burn" tells about a really hard breakup. Usher told VH1 he based the song on his own life. "You've gotten attached, you love that person. . . . It didn't work, so it burns."

> "No one can really explain that [bad] feeling. When you figured, 'I thought that this was my soul mate. I thought I found the person who had it. I thought I could be that person, too.' You've gotta go through something to get something, sometimes. My mom always said, 'If there were no humps in life, there would be nothing to get over.'"

Shaking Off Fears

Putting personal stories into songs is scary enough. But releasing those songs to be heard around the world? That's really scary. When Usher wrote *Confessions*, he was telling the world his secrets. Of course, not every **lyric** was 100 percent about him. Artists often sing lyrics that are about other people. Even so, this was a personal album.

"With every album, I try to better myself," Usher told Magic. com. In *Confessions*, he used honesty to better his music.

Record-Breaker

Not only was *Confessions* a hit with fans, it was a record-breaker, too! It had the highest first-week sales by a male artist. It won him all kinds of awards: best artist, best video, and best song. He did sold-out concerts. He appeared on TV shows.

Confessions spent twelve weeks at the top spot on the charts. Three number-one solo singles came from that album. Sales during the first week topped one million copies! Here, Usher is seen signing copies of a special edition of the record-breaker.

Meanwhile, *Confessions* spun off three number-one singles: "Confessions Part 2," "Yeah!" and "Burn." Together, they stormed the charts. The single "Yeah!" was really well liked. It won "Song of the Year." Radio stations all over the world played it.

Building His Acting Career

Usher never stopped working on his acting. He sang in the TV show *Gepetto*. It was a movie based on the Pinocchio story. Usher told MTV, "The Pinocchio story was something I loved as a kid."

Usher proved he could play a lot of different parts. He acted in another TV show, *The Famous Jett Jackson*. This time, he played an evil skateboarder and a computer hacker!

But his biggest acting job was for *In the Mix*. It came out in 2005. *In the Mix* is the story of a DJ (Usher) who protects a young girl. The girl's father is a mob boss. Usher's character is hired to be her bodyguard. While guarding her, he falls in love with her. Sparks fly, and there are the ups and downs of romance.

The Godson of Soul Takes a Breath

Usher had been going nonstop since he was a little kid. Most people would have burned out. Usher knew he needed to be careful. He told *People* magazine he wanted to "slow down and breathe." He needed to find balance.

But as usual, Usher still found time to perform. He was still going strong. He danced on stage with funk superstar James Brown. They performed together at the 2005 Grammys. It was a big honor just singing next to Brown. But then the superstar gave him the title "Godson of Soul." Life couldn't get much better than that!

Hip-Hop lingo

A **charity** is a group that gives time, money, skills, or other things to help people in need.

Chapter 5

Beyond the Music

Usher's goals weren't limited to music. He had dreams beyond just stardom. He also wanted to make a difference in the world. He already did that through his music. Now he wanted to do that through his **charity**. Hip-hop and charity go together well. Many of hip-hop's biggest stars give back to people.

Reaching Out to Others

Usher didn't grow up with a lot of money. He was like a lot of kids in America. But he also had a lot of help along the way. He had a mom who believed in his dream. He had role models like L.A. Reid and P. Diddy.

Many kids aren't as lucky as Usher. Kids from poor neighborhoods have it rough. Not only are they poor, but they also hear negative things all day. Very few positive messages get sent to poor kids. They're told that they should give up. They're told that they'll always be poor.

Usher wanted to be a positive role model. As early as 1999, Usher started charity work. Remember that Usher was only twenty-one years old at that point. But he already knew he wanted to help. So he held a three-day fan club. He invited Puff Daddy, Jermaine Dupri, and the Atlanta Falcons football team. The event raised a lot of money for kids who were at risk of ending up in trouble.

He's also done charity work to keep kids in school. After the terrorist attacks on September 11, 2001, he also helped raise money for victims. And in 2002, he helped raise money to fight AIDS. He raised money after Hurricane Katrina, too. He created Project Restart. Its goal was to help families find new homes after Katrina.

A Helping Hand

Clearly, Usher has done some big, public charity work. But what about the small, everyday stuff? In January 2000, Usher was driving near Atlanta when he came across a burning car. A woman had escaped, but her clothes were on fire. Usher pulled over and tried to help her. He put out the flames with his jacket. Then he waited with her for the ambulance.

Sadly, the woman died a few weeks later. But her son was grateful to Usher. He called a radio station to thank Usher publicly.

More Musical Gold

Usher still had a lot of music up his sleeve. In 2008, he released the album *Here I Stand*. As usual, it was a hit. The single "Love In This Club" went straight to number one. It was one of the fastest-selling songs of Usher's career.

In 2010, Usher released his next album, *Raymond v. Raymond*. Fans hadn't seemed to like *Here I Stand* as much as other albums. So Usher really turned up the heat on *Raymond*. In 2007, Usher had married Tameka Foster. Sadly, the couple only lasted two years. They divorced in 2009. Many of the songs on *Raymond* are about their failed love. In August, 2010, Usher released *Versus*, a short album of songs left off of *Raymond v. Raymond*.

The Future

For Usher, it's still just the beginning. He sees his career going well into the future. His musical talent doesn't seem to have an end. And his acting career is in full swing. Also, he continues to take young talent under his wing. He helped Justin Bieber become a huge success. Usher signed a contract with him in 2008. By 2010, Bieber was a megastar. Today, he's one of the biggest artists in music.

Usher kept working on his own music, too. In 2012, he put out a song called "Climax." The slow song is about the end of a relationship. Usher said that the song would be on his next album.

After years in the music business, Usher still feels confident. He told MTV, "I'll keep going in the right direction, as long as I keep my head in the sky, keep a positive attitude, and do what I love."

Usher's future seems unlimited. Though he has hinted at early retirement from performing, he shows no sign of letting up anytime soon. Whether it's music, business, film, or charity, there's clearly much more of Usher to come.

1978   Usher Raymond IV is born in Dallas, Texas, on October 14.

1994   Usher records first album for LaFace Records.

1996   Usher contributes a song to the 1996 Olympics' tribute album.

1997   Usher makes his acting debut as Jeremy on *Moesha*.

He receives a Grammy nomination.

Second album, *My Way*, is released.

He performs at the Apollo Theater in New York City.

He tours as opening act on Puff Daddy's No Way Out tour.

1998   Usher creates his own record label, Us Records.

He makes his film debut as a high school student possessed by aliens in *The Faculty*.

He's named *Billboard* Entertainer of the Year

He receives nomination for Best Male R&B Vocal Performance.

He's selected one of the "21 Hottest Stars Under 21" by *Teen People*.

He tours as opening act for Mary J. Blige.

He wins Soul Train Music Award for "You Make Me Wanna . . .".

He tours as opening act for Janet Jackson's Velvet Rope tour.

1999   NAACP awards Usher the Image Award for Outstanding Actor in a Daytime Drama Series in recognition of his work on *The Bold and the Beautiful* in June 1998.

He records "How Much" with Mariah Carey.

Usher Live, recorded at a free concert in Chattanooga, is released.

He hosts a three-day fan club convention.

2000   Usher appears in the film *Texas Rangers*.

He costars in television special *Geppetto*.

2001   Usher performs at the United We Stand benefit concert in Washington, D.C.

He releases *8701*.

2002   Usher performs at the "Staying Alive" concert in South Africa.

He wins Best Male R&B Vocal Award at the Grammy's.

He participates in the 17th Annual Magic Johnson's "A Midsummer Night's Magic" charity event.

He begins dating Rozonda "Chilli" Thomas of TLC.

2003   Usher becomes only the third artist to win back-to-back Grammys as Best Male R&B Vocal.

2004   His album *Confessions* sells a record-breaking 1.1 million in its first week of release, and he has his first simultaneous number-one pop and number-one R&B singles.

He wins eleven *Billboard* Awards.

2005   Usher costars in *the Mix*

James Brown calls Usher the "Godson of Soul" at the Grammy Awards.

He purchases part ownership of the Cleveland Cavaliers of the NBA.

He starts Project Restart to aid victims of the Gulf Coast hurricanes.

2006   Usher stars in and produces the film *The Ballad of Walter Homes.*

2007   Usher marries his long-time stylist and girlfriend, Tameka Foster.

2008   Usher releases his fifth studio album, *Here I Stand.*

2009   Usher files for divorce from his wife, Tameka Foster.

2010   Usher releases two studio albums, *Raymond v. Raymond,* and *Versus.*

Discography
Albums

1994	Usher
1997	My Way
1999	Live
2001	Confessions
	Confessions–Special Edition
2008	Here I Stand
2010	Raymond v. Raymond
2010	Versus

Number-One Singles

1998	"Nice and Slow"
2001	"U Got It Bad"
	"U Remind Me"
2004	"My Boo" (with Alicia Keys)
	"Confessions 2"
	"Burn"
	"Yeah!" (with Lil John and Ludacris)
2008	"Love in This Club" (with Young Jeezy)
2010	"OMG" (with will.i.am)

In Books

Adams, Colleen. *Usher*. New York: PowerKids Press, 2006.

Horn, Geoffrey M. *Usher*. New York: Gareth Stevens, 2005.

Masar, Brenden. *Usher*. Farmington Hills, Mich.: Lucent, 2006.

Nickson, Chris. *Usher: The Godson of Soul*. New York: Simon Spotlight, 2005.

Torres, John Albert. *Usher*. Hockessin, Del.: Mitchell Lane, 2005.

Whitcombe, Dan. *Usher*. Chicago: Heinemann-Raintree, 2005.

Websites

AOL Music Usher Page
music.aol.com/artist/usher

Starpulse Usher Page
www.starpulse.com/Music/Usher

Usher's New Look Foundation
www.ushersnewlook.org

Usher's Official Website
www.usherworld.com

Index

About the Author

Z.B. Hill is a an author and publicist living in Binghamton, New York. He has a special interest in adolescent education and how music can be used in the classroom.

Picture Credits

Ace Pictures/Kristin Callahan: p. 38
Brian Prahl/Splash News: p. 32
Dimitri Halkidis/WENN: p. 8
Dreamstime, Sbukely: p. 1
Everett Collection: p. 20
KRT/NMI: p. 34
KRT/Tim Grant: p. 36
Miramax Films/NMI: p. 22
PRNewsFoto/NMI: p. 30, 41
Robyn Mackenzie: p. 6
Shannon McCollum/WENN: p. 17
Zuma Press/Nancy Kaszerman: p. 11
Zuma Press/Rahav Segev: p. 28
Zuma Press/Steven Tackeff: p. 14, 18, 24
Zuma Press/URH/UPPA: p. 26

To the best knowledge of the publisher, all other images are in the public domain. If any image has been inadvertently uncredited, please notify Harding House Publishing Services, Vestal, New York 13850, so that rectification can be made for future printings.